THE MAKING

Ben Freeman Jr.
2015

Scripture verses depicting KJV, NASB and NLT are taken from the
E-Sword Copyright 2000-2014, Rick Meyers
www.e-sword.net/support.html. All Rights Reserved.
&
Bible Explorer 4.0, Copyright 2006, WORDsearch
http://.bible-explorer.com. All Rights Reserved.

The Making
Copyright © 2015 by Ben Freeman Jr.
www.greatlineage.com
ben@greatlineage.com

ISBN 978-0-9966083-0-5
Library of Congress Control Number 2015948032

Published by
Rapier Publishing Company
360 W. Main Street, Suite #1
Dothan, Alabama 36301

www.rapierpublishing.com
Facebook: www.rapierpublishing@gmail.com
Twitter: rapierpublishing@rapierpub

Printed in the United States of America
All rights reserved under the International Copyright Law. Contents and/or cover may not be reproduced in whole or in part in any form without the consent of the Publisher, or Author.

Book Cover Design/ Book Layout: Rapture Graphics

The views expressed in this work are solely those of the author and do not necessarily reflect the views of the publisher, and the publisher hereby disclaims any responsibility for them.

Any people depicted in the imagery provided by the illustrator are models, and such illustrations or art are being used for illustrative purposes only. Illustrations are created by Garrett Myers. Visit him at garrettmyersart@gmail.com

Andrew Smiley created the Potter's Hands artwork.

DEDICATION

I have the honor of dedicating my book, "The Making" to my wife, Robyn, the one and only woman that has been there with me through this whole process. I can honestly say I couldn't have done it without you. I thank you, and I Love You. I also want to dedicate "The Making" to you, the reader. Thank you for purchasing "The Making", and may you be blessed because of it. I want to also encourage you to read it from start to finish. I want you to know just how important it is to continue in your process of growing up and living your life in Christ while being an individual.

To you, from me,

Ben

"But You
O' Child of God, flee from all evil things; and pursue righteousness, godliness, faith, love, patience, and gentleness. Because Thou are my Beloved, I pray above all things that you may prosper and be in good health, just as your soul prospers. Remember, you did not choose Me, but I chose you and I appointed you that you should go and bear fruit, and that your fruit should remain, that whatever you ask the Father in My name He may give you. So "Take heed to the ministry which you have received from the Lord, that you may fulfill it." (1st Timothy 6:11, 3 John 1:2, John 15:16, Colossians 4:17)

Table of Contents

Introduction...7

I **The Relationship**..9

   1. My Wife and I...11

   2. Hear My Cry...15

   3. Butt Praise unto You..19

   4. The Image..25

   5. Here and There..35

   6. Stop Playing..41

   7. Look Straight..45

   8. Despite...49

   9. One and Onlys..51

   10. One Purpose...55

   11. Two of a Kind...61

   12. Three Way Love Affair..................................65

   13. The Ultimate Relationship...........................69

II **The Minister**..73

   14. The Cost..75

15. The Hand You Have 77

16. Know Your Moment 81

III The Great Comeback **89**

17. Why Believe 91

18. Your Great Comeback 93

IV Conversation Starter **97**

••• WWJD 1G 📶   9:11 AM   100% 🔋
< Author   **INTRODUCTION**   Reader

- Hey!
- Hello!
- I got a book for you to read!
- What's it about?
- Men and Women...
- Really???
- Some of it is funny & challenging. You will find some of it is eye opening
- OH?
- Oh Yea, you will find what I Call Huddle-Up where you and someone else can talk about what you have read. Also, You'll find Hit and Runs, Where I hit on certain topics ... and keep going
- That's cool!
- I believe you will enjoy it.
- Whatever?
-

THE RELATIONSHIP

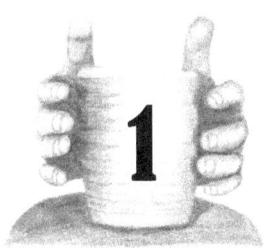

My Wife and I

For those that don't know me, my wife and I have five wonderful kids. In the beginning, we both had different mindsets when it came to having children.

When my wife first told me that we were pregnant with our first child, my first thoughts were, *"OK, I've got nine months to plan this out. I have to have somewhere for "IT" to sleep, provide food for "IT" to eat and ways for "IT" to be clean."* Then I was thinking, *"OK, I don't want to be around everyone, so I need to be far enough away from people (where they would have to give me a heads up before they come), and close enough to where if I needed a babysitter, I can call them and they could come."* This was my mindset.

Her mindset was, *"Yay, I'm pregnant! He or she will be here in 9 months!"* She went down the list *"Month 1: I will feel like this. Month 2: I will feel like that and by month 3 I should feel and think…"*

In my mind, I was *"Planning for War in a Time of Peace."* In her mind, it was *"It's Happening Now"*. I say all of this to say,

The Making

that you can be in the same situation with someone and have two entirely different mindsets. For example, like me, I was so close to the situation that I couldn't see *the forest for the trees*. *I didn't believe that her morning sickness was more important than finding a place to stay.*

This caused problems early on in our relationship. If I had taken the time to think about how differently we were wired, or how I was thinking, I would have been able to see how easily we could have worked together.

But I didn't.

So we didn't.

Even though, we were having this child and thinking that we were on one accord, we were actually working against one another because we did not want the same thing (in each other's minds anyway).

Take note when people say, "Well in my mind" or "In my mind I was thinking…" When someone says this, he or she is almost 90% wrong about what the other person is thinking or talking about.

> *"Take note when people say, "Well in my mind" or "In my mind I was thinking…" When someone says this, he or she is almost 90% wrong about what the other person is thinking or talking about."*

So in my mind she didn't care where "IT" lived, where "IT" slept, what "IT" wore, what and how much "IT" ate, or even where the food would come from to feed "IT". I could not believe her. She was just *soooooooo…* happy to be pregnant. She was happy about how her body was changing and feeling. *She Was Something Else!* She completely overlooked all the mental hard work I was doing and all the things I was planning.

In my mind, she didn't care. I felt she was looking down on me. This created another problem because now she was hitting my manhood by looking down on me. All of this was going on in my head because of my tendency to be a perfectionist, which only made things worse. On top of that, I was keeping it all inside. I was thinking to myself, "*She should be happy I'm doing all this for her. Another woman would love for her man to be doing this for her.*" This created another problem because I was convincing myself that she was not grateful for what I was doing for her and that someone else would be grateful.

Can you see how my mind was getting the best of me? This was our first kid. This should have been a time of joy. We should have been enjoying the time and experiencing a special sense of togetherness, but it wasn't. It became another assignment to do. It was like two people at work working on the same project, but couldn't see eye to eye because they weren't looking at each other or working together.

In the end, my wife and I had to learn that we had to get on the same page about this baby thing. She was talking, but I wasn't hearing. I was doing, but she was talking. I was thinking to myself, but she couldn't read my mind. In order for us to work together, we had to communicate. Communicating takes both people talking and listening to one another about their feelings, anticipations, needs, and yes, fears. We had to develop a mindset of "making it work". That became one of our goals, "to make it work".

The Making

In order for any relationship to work, you have you to set a goal to have a "making it work" kind of mindset. The goal should be for both of you to come to a mutual agreement. You know, like two people who have settled on a matter and they shake hands – right hand to right hand – in agreement becoming goal and focused oriented, creating an environment of teamwork for the benefit of the outcome. Both are right in what they are doing; and, as a result, they are working together like hands fitting together in agreement, complimenting each other.

To meet this goal for yourselves, you and your spouse will have to learn how to work through things while making it work. It is up to you to figure out the best way to work together and the best way to get the job done as quickly as possible so that you can enjoy the precious times in your life.

Hear My Cry

I'll start with this analogy:

There was a certain woman that had a two-year-old little boy. This mom was a good mom who always finished what she started. Now, her son, Allen was at the age of potty training. His mom had been working with him teaching him all the warning signs of using the bathroom like a big boy.

Then, one day as usual, they both were home and everything was going great until Allen felt all the warning signs come alive in his body. He did everything that his mother had told him.

She had told him to come to her whenever he had an "urge" so she could take him to the bathroom. He did just that when he had an "urge" to go to the bathroom. He went to her and said, *"Momma, momma, I need to go. I need you to help me. I need you, momma!"* She was washing dishes while talking on the phone with her friend, and they were talking about their *Soaps* that were on at that time. Tapping her on the leg, little Allen said, *"Momma, momma I need to go. I need you to help me. I need you, momma."* She couldn't hear him because her mind was somewhere else.

The Making

So, Allen did what he knew to do. He went into the bathroom and fiddled with his pants, running in place, trying to get them unfastened. While struggling with his pants, he lost control and let it loose, unwillingly. He didn't make it in time and knew he had messed up. Allen went back to his mother and told her what he had done. Now when his mom saw this, she was very disappointed and said, *"Allen, why did you wet your pants? We've been over this time and time. You should have told me that you needed me and I would have taken you."* She popped him on the bottom and said, *"This is a no-no!"*

Unfortunately, this happens often in relationships. When someone in authority or a position such as, a husband, wife, mommy or daddy is wrapped up in doing his or her own thing, he or she completely overlooks the other person and their responsibility to that person. Many times, the person can't even see that it was his or her fault that the other person messed up. They punish the other person by using guilt, the silent treatment, or worse calling them names outside their character. In some cases, like Allen's, he wasn't old enough to say, *"No momma, I did. I did tell you I needed you."*

Most of the time, people like the momma in this analogy would not listen to Allen because he's too young and immature. This happens in relationships when one person have an advantage over another and thinks they know more because they have proven themselves to be more knowledgeable in areas whereas the other is not.

I believe we all have been in situations like Allen's every now and then. A husband or wife can say to the other, *"Baby, I need you to listen to me and talk to me; we need to talk. I have something going on in me that I can't fully explain, but if you don't pay me any attention right now I'm going to make a mess of myself, either with someone or something. Help me. I need you."* Another example is when one spouse becomes suspicious of someone the other spouse has contact with, either through work, or friendship. The spouse would say, *"Babe, I don't think you should be around that person. I have a bad feeling about this person. I can't prove the situation to be wrong, I've just got a bad feeling and I want you to be on guard or out of the situation."* But the other spouse doesn't listen or take heed of the warning. Unfortunately, this happens in many relationships. One spouse may think he or she knows it all but then ends up falling. They thought they were in control, and that they had the situation under control.

It is in these moments, that we believe we have already done the main things, such as talking to a marriage counselor before we got married, or because we had what looks like a good upbringing, we think we would know what to do in a time of need.

As with Allen's mother, because of the perceived preparation and training, we tend to think to ourselves, "Hey, things are good!" Things are fine, or at least they look fine." When we've been over every drill there is in marriage, we say things like, "If they need something they'll ask." But often they don't, and we don't either. We sit there expecting things to change, or for someone to notice our need. Unfortunately, that's how we ruin our relationships. We believe that the other person already knows our needs; after all, they see us every day.

Over the years my wife and I have learned the importance of confessing our confessions. We use the "Life and Power" that is in our tongues to create the world around us (our lives) to be like we want it to be. God taught us through His Word to do this. Therefore, we took the same principle and applied it to our marriage. I'm not saying that we are perfect, but things are a lot better than they use to be when we were just sitting there expecting something to happen without saying anything. We have learned to communicate our concerns with one another despite what may be going on around us or how we may feel at the time. *(By understanding that we are all human, and we all have needs, no matter how big or small one may be, we have to voice it to one another.)*

We have to learn how to take a second and really think about the message and reason someone is trying to instruct or guide us; many lifelong problems could be avoided if we do. As adults, we are often faced with problems that could have been avoided if someone had cared enough to speak up, or if we had listened when someone did speak up. Our life problems and difficult situations do not just wash away as if we just "peed" on ourselves like Allen.

> *"By understanding that we are all human and we all have needs, no matter how big or small one may be, we have to voice it to one another."*

The decision is ours. Whoever may be crying out, take a second to listen and see what their tears are all about.

Butt Praise unto You

⁶ Now it had happened as they were coming *home,* when David was returning from the slaughter of the Philistine, that the women had come out of all the cities of Israel, singing and dancing, to meet King Saul, with tambourines, with joy, and with musical instruments. ⁷ So the women sang as they danced, and said: "Saul has slain his thousands, And David his ten thousands." 1 Samuel 18:6-7 (NKJV)

Butt **Praise** is praise that comes from outsiders that is directed to someone close to you. It's flattering and flirting to them, but taunting and threatening to you, which can cause you to feel livid, scared, and helpless on the inside.

⁸ "Then Saul was very angry, and the saying displeased him; and he said, "They have ascribed to David ten thousands, and to me they have ascribed *only* thousands. Now *what* more can he have but the kingdom?" 1 Samuel 18:8 (NKJV)

What Saul was feeling is also known as jealousy.

⁹ "So Saul eyed David from that day forward." 1 Samuel 18:9 (NKJV)

The Making

Has anyone ever uplifted your mate so much that it made you feel uncomfortable? It was like they were hitting on them to the point that you thought, "*Do you want to go get a room or something?*" or "*It's obvious to me that if I wasn't here you would be next in line?*" Or, how about this one, "*I don't see how you ended up with this person.*" Confronted with these thoughts digs at a person and provokes jealousy.

The King vs. The Armor Bearer

Let's look back at Saul and David. They both were doing what they were assigned to do. Saul was appointed by God to be King, and then Saul chose David to be his armor bearer (1 Samuel 16:21). For Saul to feel slighted, or taunted, by David's accomplishments would be a natural thing to happen; after all, David was a servant of the king. He was inferior to the King, yet David's deed was exalted over that of Saul's deed.

The Singer vs. The Usher

When it came to Robyn and me, we have had some major differences. Her family was big on education; whereas, my family was big on being self-sufficient. They taught me how to take care of myself, clean up after myself, look-out for myself, learn a trade that you can work and make your own money, and to manage myself well. Robyn was taught that education was the key to your success. I was taught that I was the key to my success. Fortunately for us, we were raised in the church, so we knew that Jesus was the head of our life, but we also knew we had to take responsibility for our lives.

Butt Praise unto You Two

We would be in church and my beautiful wife would be in the choir, just singing and praising the Lord with all her friends, both men ☹ and women ☺.

The Relationship

At first it was cool and I was thankful, but then one too many people would come up to me afterwards praising her, telling me how pretty her smile was and how lucky of a man I was to have a woman like her. Sometimes we would be at the mall and people I didn't know were just *too* head over heels about my wife.

PAUSE: Robyn was doing everything right. My wife was a great teacher; all the students liked her. She was faithful to the church, and she sang in the choir. So why was I so uncomfortable and jealous?

PLAY: Because they liked the one I loved. They were, in my mind, beginning to fall for the one that I fell in love with and there was nothing I could do about it. I couldn't explain or justify why I wanted her to stop. I thought to myself: who am I to stop her from doing God's Will for her life. I would tell myself we are supposed to Praise Him. We are supposed to work. So why then am I feeling so mad?

On top of all this, people were complimenting her, and this made her feel good. I would tell myself compliments are supposed to make her feel good about herself. That's what they do for you. So, here I am with this great wife that everyone knows and likes, and I am over in the corner steaming and nitpicking everything she did, completely teed off in the church. At home, I had turned into a grumpy young man, looking at my wife do the Will of God for her life, and thinking to myself, how dare her to be so happy while I'm so unhappy. After I had calmed down, I asked God, *"What do you do when your praise can't amount to the praise of so many others? I couldn't see how I could make her feel like everyone else was making her feel. There's no feeling like that.* I would think to myself, "How are we going

The Making

to make this marriage work?" Everyone was making her out to be so big and great while I was feeling so small. No one likes to feel small, especially men.

Now to flip the coin, because before we start answering those questions let me tell you what my wife encountered. I was the young guy on the block. At church, I was the new usher with all the kids. I was the young man serving the Lord while leading his family. Robyn was in the same boat as me. She was cool with everything at first. However, once she'd notice that I was being noticed, and they (meaning women) started noticing that she wasn't with me, and I was doing it alone, and they began to notice what kind of guy I was, she didn't like how it made her feel either. When she was out and about, women would walk up to her and tell her how well I handled the kids and how well-behaved they were and how good I did it alone. They would say things like, "I wish my man was like that," or "I wish I had a man like that," to her face, and this was the beginning of her Butt Praise unto me Experience.

I was known as the young usher with all the kids, and she was known as the singing teacher. We both were doing what we knew to do. I loved taking care of my kids and helping out at church, and she loved singing in the choir and teaching. So what should we do if we were both doing what we knew and enjoyed? While we were growing closer to God and His people, it was driving us further and further apart from each other. We were almost to the point of just tolerating each other until it was time for us to either go to work or go to church, as long as it was away from each other. We both felt alone in our marriage while feeling alive everywhere else.

This kind of Praise will cause all the fears and symptoms of a troubled marriage to begin to pop up. As men, we tend to get aggressive and dominating like a lost animal that can't find its way. Women often begin to feel intimidated by little things and become fearful. Men and women, both, can be put under stress and begin to fall apart on the inside while looking around on the outside.

So how does one handle this kind of Praise? Mainly, if fear is causing thoughts like: "I think you may leave me if you find someone else bigger and better than me," or how can one tell the other, "*I'm feeling neglected and I need some attention, but you are always gone.*"

What Robyn and I had to do was admit that we had a problem and why that problem existed. We had to voice our fears to one another. I had to tell her how I felt when people were coming up to me telling me "*what I got*" as if I didn't know what I had. She had to do the same. We had to tell each other about our fears of others falling for what we fell in love with. I felt other men were coveting my wife. Robyn felt other women were coveting her husband. We both felt that others were coveting us individually and not the attributes of our relationship. We were afraid that other people would fall for what we saw in each other, and they would desire to have one or the other of us as "*their ideal mate*". The fear was that we could be replaced. Robyn and I had to recognize the importance of each other's thoughts and emotions. We had to keep in mind that this could not be fixed overnight. We had to work together and not tell the other that you don't have anything to worry about, I'm good.

Butt praise can come to anyone doing anything, at anytime or anywhere. It can come from family members, coaches, teammates, fans, students or classmates, or anybody in any occupation. In regard to this type of praise, we have to beware of this Praise. We have to make sure that we are not taking it in or giving it out.

The Image

When it comes to relationships, people say that opposites attract, but in the "moment" when we first meet, we don't always recognize our differences that make us opposites. At the time, we want the same stuff, and we feel the same way. We all know that as times change, moments change and people change. There are many great books out there that talk about that kind of stuff, but what I would like to share in this section is my opinion on three of the hardest things for a married man to keep the same when everything else is changing around him. I will be speaking about life changing moments from my personal experiences. Like how I saw things, how I walked through them, and how I got over them. I've learned from personal experience and conversations with others that a good man or woman can be easily broken, but hard to fix, especially by the hands of the person that hurt or broke them. I am going to go from 3-2-1 (get it) 3 to 1. ☺

The 3rd hardest thing for a man to do is to cry out to a woman (his wife) when he is in need. It's hard for a man to talk to her about his emotions

> *"A good man or woman can be easily broken, but hard to fix, especially by the hands of the person that hurt or broke them."*

The Making

or anything else along those lines. It is hard for a man to lift up his robe to show himself to anyone. Mainly to those who look up to him. But I will tell you this, he will tell someone, and unfortunately it may be someone, such as a lady friend whether she is someone in his present or from his past. Why? Because he doesn't have to lose anything if they just laugh and walk away from him, or stop talking to him, because their opinions really don't matter. To him, their praises matter but their overall disappointments don't.

Something I would always tell myself and that is, if a person doesn't know my middle name, they don't really know me. Therefore, their opinion of me doesn't count. Now that may sound a little rough and tough but this is a way I would speak to myself so that I wouldn't take what someone may say to me or about me to heart. In a marriage, or in other relationships, it's easy to take what someone says to heart. The words of others, especially those close to you, can literally weigh heavy on your mind and on your heart. Those words can lead to someone getting hurt, which will ultimately result in un-forgiveness – and un-forgiveness can affect a relationship. This is where neglect can be birthed. Neglect is a big problem for many relationships, because you can't see it until it is grown, and once it's grown, it has developed legs that are ready and willing to walk right out of the relationship with no hope in sight. Once you begin to feel neglected, tell your mate immediately. They may not understand at first, but just tell them. You need to say, "When you do that, I feel like this. So, I need you to stop, or we need to come up with a plan for things to change."

I encourage you to speak up for yourself. If you are married, you owe it to yourselves to take care of one another. This book is to make you think. It doesn't have all the answers for your relationship; however, I believe it is a start. So many relationships are destroyed because someone didn't think. They didn't take a step back to think their actions or comments all the way through.

As we continue on, the 2nd hardest thing for a man to do is to keep himself for one woman, as my wife would say it with an echoing voice, **FOREVER…**

We are more than conquerors; therefore, we like to conquer things. Unfortunately, women happen to be one of those things; conquering makes us feel good. Is it wrong? Yes! I'm not justifying the way men are, by any means.

I'm just letting you know why some men do and like certain things. This may not be relatable to you or your mate. If you're a woman, ask your mate, "What do you think is something that's hard for a man to do?" If you're a man, ask yourself, "What is something that's hard for me to do?" This tendency of men to be a conqueror is correctable. There is hope for a good man. A man wants to be good to his woman; he would love to be faithful to you. He would love to be everything that you need. Unfortunately, a lot of us weren't taught at an early age the necessary life lessons that are needed later on in life. Here are two Scriptures found in the Bible that speak to men and women. Let's start with women:

⁴ "That they admonish the young women to love their husbands, to love their children, ⁵ To be discreet, chaste, homemakers, good, obedient to their own husbands, that the word of God may not be blasphemed." Titus 2:4-5 (NKJV)

You may be asking yourself, "What does that have to do

with anything?" Has anyone ever read that to you?
Now the man:

² "That the older men be sober, reverent, temperate, sound in faith, in love, in patience." Titus 2:2 (NKJV)

The #1 hardest thing for a man to do is to admit that he CAN'T. Saying "I can't" is by far the hardest thing for a man to do. I'll start with myself. About five years ago I was challenged with letting go of something that I didn't know at the time was very valuable to me. At first, I thought to myself, why do I have to do let it go? Secondly, I thought, well if I have to, I'll just do it, but first let me see what it's all about first and then I'll get rid of it in my own timing.

My "something" was a relationship. It was a friend of mine. It was a friend from the past. A person I would look to for help. Someone who understood me and made me feel free to be me. A friend that was standing smack dab in the middle of God's place in my life. I had to learn that God was the *One* that was supposed to make me feel like I was more than a conqueror. He is the *One* I should run to when I was in trouble or need. He is the *One* that heals my hurts and fills my voids. He is the *One* that makes me – me. He is the *One* that completes me. He is the *One*, not a person, not a drug, not a drink, not a place or a job, only God. Him and Him alone!

So, when it came down to me giving up that relationship, I didn't even know it was a problem. I didn't have a clue that this past relationship was a problem until God pointed it out to me. I hadn't spoken with her or thought of her. I was just living my life, and she was living hers. Now I can see how if God hadn't pointed it out to me, it would have destroyed my life later.

People are funny. We see other people's problems so easy, and have no clue that we have a bigger problem than them.

³ "And why do you look at the speck in your brother's eye, but do not consider the plank in your own eye? ⁴ Or how can you say to your brother, 'Let me remove the speck from your eye'; and look, a plank *is* in your own eye? ⁵ Hypocrite! First remove the plank from your own eye, and then you will see clearly to remove the speck from your brother's eye." Matthew 7:3-5 (NKJV)

It's so easy to point fingers. It's so easy to throw stones. It's so easy to laugh when someone else falls. It's so easy!!! That is, until we're that person. Until we're the one that has center stage and others are at the judgment table. Here is where we find out for ourselves that it's easy to fall, but hard to get back up. Here is where we find out how hard things really are.

But back to me, I had everything. I had the beautiful wife, with beautiful kids, a great paying job, a big house and a great Church that we attended. Almost everything a man can ask for I had, that's why I didn't even know I had a problem.

¹ "Because you say, 'I am rich, have become wealthy, and have need of nothing'--and do not know that you are wretched, miserable, poor, blind, and naked." Revelation 3:17 (NKJV)

I can remember saying to God, "I know you want this from me, but I don't know how to give it to you." It was like having something stuck on my back, and I needed someone else to get it off for me. Here is where I began to feel helpless. I would

The Making

think to myself, "*My Father wants something from me but I don't know how to give it to Him. If He would just tell me how, I'll give it to Him myself.*" However, what I believe He wanted from me was for me to realize was just how far off I really was. He wanted me to know just how badly I needed Him as my Savior, and not a person. Even though I was raised in a Church my whole life and serving in a Church, I didn't know this because I thought I was doing all the right things.

What does all of this have to do with the #1 hardest thing for a man to do? Everything. I had to admit that, even though I served in a good Church, had a beautiful house, beautiful kids and a beautiful wife, I had to admit that I was about to lose it all because I didn't have God in the center of my life. I was about to lose my house, divorce my wife, and lose my kids, all to the devil because he was waiting on me to get off post. I was about to leave my Church, all because of an addiction. I was addicted to having a *person* in God's spot. I was addicted to running to a *person* when I was in need. I would let a *person* dictate my future. Me being with her outweighed everything that God had given me and every person He connected me to. It was in the way of everything He wanted to give to me. Even though I wanted everything God had for me, I had gotten to a place in my life where I stopped caring, either I had it or I didn't, It didn't make a difference to me. At first, it was scary but as time went by I stopped caring to the point that all I wanted was to be with that *person.*

Now we all got a thing that can easily take God's place in our lives and amazingly enough it's a small thing that takes up a "Big" spot in our life. It can be as small as a shot glass full of our favorite drink, or small as a joint, a needle, a little white lie, the #1 meal at our favorite fast food restaurant, a little plastic card, a text in our phone, anything, a pet or a job. No matter what it may be, we have to realize the need to get it out of His spot in our lives.

> *"Amazingly enough it's a small thing that takes up a "Big" spot in our life."*

It's amazing to me how something so small can outweigh or replace something so big in our life. You may have seen it with your own eyes, either on TV or in your family. How someone decided to keep a bad habit and pretty much said forget the rest. In my own life, I can remember saying, "God I thank you for all that you have given me. I know it all came from You and How much You love me and how You died on the cross for me." But, I didn't care. Why? Because my heart was so entwined with hers that I couldn't get free on my own. I couldn't just walk away as if nothing was there. I had to admit that I couldn't get free. It was like wearing a straitjacket. I tried to do everything in my might to get untwined but I was stuck; yet, I pictured myself free. I told myself I didn't have a problem; I'll get out of this soon. "I'm good!" Still, as time went on and things began to become noticeable to others, I struggled even the more.

My Imaginary Problem

In my mind, I could tell people were talking about my family and me; so I started talking too, to get them to see what was really going on. Because this is what we do when we can't stop a *thing*. We make it look good. We make running women look good. We make drinking look good. We make eating all kinds of foods look good. We make not taking care of our kids look good. *And* if making whatever it is look good don't work, we blame. We blame the women, we blame our friends, we blame our parents, or we blame the church. We even go as far as blaming God. We say things like, He made me like this; He knew I

The Making

couldn't stop. Then we get into groups and say things like, it's their fault we are in need and we can't do whatever it is that we are trying to do. It's everyone else's fault that I can't. Here is an example found in John 5.

> [5] "One of the men lying there had been sick for thirty-eight years. [6] When Jesus saw him and knew he had been ill for a long time, he asked him, "Would you like to get well?" [7] "I can't, sir," the sick man said, "for I have no one to put me into the pool when the water bubbles up. Someone else always gets there ahead of me." [8] Jesus told him, "Stand up, pick up your mat, and walk!" John 5:5-8 (NLT)

We do things to keep the responsibility off ourselves. We'll do whatever it takes to make ourselves look good because we know that we can't stop ourselves from doing _____ and because we can't **stop**, we don't **stop**. I am not saying that just because you choose the Lord, everything will be fine. I'm not saying that because once you get Him on your side, now you're accountable for your actions. You should know better. Now you have accepted the calling to be made.

As we wrap up the hardest things for a man to do, I want you to consider the moral of the story, which is to come to grips with admitting that we have a problem and we really can't stop if we wanted to; even though, we know what we are doing may be killing us.

There are steps we can take in overcoming the hard *thing* we find ourselves confronted with and put a stop to the Image of I'm good and we're O.K.

- We have to admit that something on the inside of us

loves whatever it is we do.
- We have to realize that yes it is in God's spot in our lives.
- We can't remove it on our own.
- We are in need of our Savior.

Remember these and apply them to the *thing* that is stealing your joy and taking away from your relationship with God.

Here and There

Isn't it a good feeling when you know that you have someone who is there for you? Someone you can call when you need to talk, someone you can talk to when you don't know what to do, or just someone you can share your good news. The Bible says that God is with us and that He will never leave nor forsake us. He is always with us; therefore, we are never alone.

We were made to be relational. We are made to look at someone and have an emotional, mental or physical reaction with them. Even in our relationship with God, we should have some kind of exchange, whether it's spiritual or mental, there should be an exchange. There are things that should be expected when one is in a relationship.

What do you think I am trying to point out here with this *Here and There* stuff...? The importance of it!!! Do we really understand the importance of our presence to our family, friends, mate, children, employees, employer, church, church members or whoever are connected to us? Just how important are we and how do we affect the *Here and There* needs in relationships.

The Right to Be There

The thing about being *there* for someone is to let him or her know that they are just as important to you as you are to them. No one wants to be in a lopsided relationship, where you have one person more involved and committed than the other. What we do want to know is that we are both in this relationship together and no one or nothing else can take our place. Just the thought of having someone *there* for you can change almost any situation.

Early in my marriage I told Robyn, "Babe, life for me right now is like walking down a dark alley where I can't see anything but a glimpse of light 200 feet in front of me."

She looked at me and said, "Ben, I don't have a clue what you are talking about. How can life be like a dark alley?"

Going on, I said, "I don't have a clue where God is taking us, but I do believe that if we keep going and make it to the light (which is Jesus) everything will be brighter to us." I went on to tell her that it made me feel good to know that she was the *here* with me. I needed her to know the importance of her being by my side. I, also, needed her to know the importance of her not complaining, not judging our current situation, and not looking back to what once was- just *here is all I needed*.

I didn't need her being my GPS trying to tell me which way to go, or a body guard to protect me. I am a man. I can fend for myself. I can see the light for myself. I could see the fear in her eyes, the insecurity in her expression, and the disappointment she felt because of what I was saying. I told her, "Just try and stay cool. What I need is for you to be *here* with me and chill out."

It was important to me to be able to hear God's voice, and if she was talking and complaining, I couldn't concentrate or hear myself think. I could'nt hear His Voice. All I needed was for her to just be *there*, and by her just being there that was all the help I needed.

I had to remind myself, and Robyn, to not worry about what's going on over *there* with our family or over *there* with our friends, but to take care of what's going on over *here* — with us and our kids. I would remind Robyn that it always made me feel good to know that she was *here* with me and that being without her is like being in a house when it is pitch black at night all alone. Have you ever had that feeling? The feeling you got when you were young and afraid of the dark, or when walking through someone else's house, or a new building looking for something alone?

Have you ever had that uneasy feeling, but then, once someone is with you it's not as bad? Matter-of-fact, you have a sense of confidence and teamwork going on. That's the feeling I would have whenever Robyn was with me and we were doing something new. I just needed her *there* with me. I believe we're all like that from time to time, but for Robyn and I, it would always happen when we were doing something new, when we were somewhere new, or new stuff was going on around us.

There will be times when we need to be alone, but just for a moment, and even in those moments it's good to know that you have someone *there* who is waiting for you to come out so you can be *there* with them. So, as you communicate your here and there needs with each other, *remember*, they need you *Here* and

The Making

There for them too; it's important that you do.

Stay from Here

As hard as it may be at times for us to always be *there* for those closest to us, it's just as easy for us to be there for people that we should never be there for.

My wife and I had a friend, way-back-when, that was a single woman — let's call her Peggy.

Peggy went to church and had a good job. The problem she had was that she worked around married men. Now, Peggy wasn't attracted to them and she respected them and their wives; however, they would talk to her, and tell her everything because they felt that they could trust her. She was a good woman and a good listener, and so she couldn't understand how other women got these good men. Our friend would tell us, *"I don't see how those women got their husbands; those wives don't even take care of their husbands."* She seemed to know everything that their wives weren't doing and everything that the husbands needed. (Now of course, she only heard their side and not their wives' side.)

There were about three men Peggy worked around who spoke to her separately so they didn't know that she knew of the others. We would tell her that she needed to cut back on talking to them, because they were going to start developing feelings for her and wanting more of her. I told her, *"Peggy, what you need to do is stop being there for them. Whenever one of them needed to talk, they will call on you and not their wives. They will look to you and not their wives every time something came up or they didn't know what to do."*

While all this was going on, Peggy wanted a man of her own. They kept telling her how good of a woman she was and how happy they were that she was always *there* for them. They would tell her how their wives were never *there* for them when they needed them to be like she was. They would go on and on about how their wives didn't understand their needs, or how they didn't show respect to them as a man, like our friend showed them.

Peggy would complain all the time about these men. She couldn't understand why she couldn't find a good man of her own. I would say," *Can't nobody get to you because you're always there for someone else. You can't see the guy right in front of you because of what is going on right there in front of you with all your married friends and their problems.*" All she had to do was pay attention to what was really going on within her. She knew what was happening but since she couldn't see the full picture, she couldn't see what was really going on. She couldn't see that she was actually hurting the marriages of these men, even though, she was trying to help the man within the marriage.

As people we live, and hopefully we learn. When it comes to being **Here and There** for people, we must know and choose the right people to share our time and lives. We must keep our priorities in line and stay away from wrong situations no matter how we may see it.

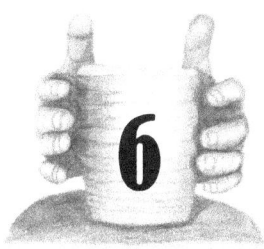

Stop Playing

Stop playing you have too much to lose

Imagine there is a couple on a rowboat in the middle of a pond. They are out there spending quality time together, when all of a sudden, the young man gets up and begins to dance for the girl in the boat. Now, they're in a small row boat so this is no place to be playing around because if one goes down into the water, it's a possibility that the other will tip over and fall into the water too. That being said, he keeps on dancing and playing around, and now low and behold, he falls in, *"SPLASH!"*

Now she is looking down at him thinking, *"You dummy! Didn't I tell you to stop playing around? I can't swim, and you are too big to pull back into the boat. What are you going to do?"* Now the man is on the verge of drowning. *"Help!"* he says as he goes up and down trying to keep his head above water. *"I can't!!!"* She cries out at the top of her lungs.

STOP This is a classic case of how sin can creep in, right when you are in the middle of doing something and ruin every-

The Making

thing. Let's take a closer look, starting at Step 1.

1. Obviously they had to be in **agreement** with one another to get in a small boat to go across a lake.

2. They couldn't swim, but they were in a boat. Meaning they were not properly taught about relationships, marriage, finances, or kids before they got into their situation.

3. The man thought he knew what he was doing. He thought he had control of the situation.

4. He wouldn't listen.

5. He fell into a bad situation that he himself couldn't get out of or control.

This can go both ways – male or female. One may think that flirting is ok or spending time with someone else is ok because it's fun or funny at the moment. One may think it's ok to stop and get a drink on the way home, text while driving or just anything else that looks unwise to do. I've been the guy in the water, and my wife has been the girl on the boat. I've been stupid and helpless, and she has been left alone and helpless.

No matter what it may be, we've got to **Stop Playing** and listen to one another. When it comes to your relationships, you have to protect them, learn from each other, know each other and keep each other accountable. I didn't finish the story about the couple in the boat on purpose. We've all made bad decisions at the wrong moment that had bad or just not the best endings. What do you think happened to the couple? What happened in your life that was similar to theirs that could have been different and had a better outcome in the end? We must always learn from the past so we won't repeat it in the future.

Look Straight

"But his wife looked back from behind him, and she became a pillar of salt." Genesis 19:26 (NLT)

I think we all have a little bit of the nature of Lot's wife in us. I know Robyn and I used to, especially in the beginning. There were times early on in our marriage that she would look on social media and see all the things her single friends were doing, and I could just see it on her face. She would look at me while the kids were crying in her ears, and I would ask her, "What's for dinner toots?" I could see her thinking to herself what happened to me? I could be at the beach with my friends or at college having fun…but????? Look at me now. What happened? I would be like, "Babe, hey Babe, I asked you a question. Are you ok?" Her face would say Noooooo, but her voice was saying, "Yeah babe, I'm good." I would be thinking, "Yeah right," while looking at the kids and thinking this woman is crazy. Then there were times when my brother would call and tell me how he was going to go and hang out with my uncles and cousins and what they were going to be doing. Then I would think to myself, "I wonder if what's her name is going to be there? I wonder what she has been up to?" Then my wife

The Making

would come up to me and say, "Babe, hey babe, what are you smiling about?" I would say, "Huh? Oh, Oh I was just thinking about how good your food is going to be Sugar Pie." After this happened a couple of times, I had to admit to her what I was really thinking, and then she would admit to me what she was thinking and we would both get angry at one another and say, "If you miss your old life so badly, you should just go." However, as Christians we had to stop doing that and act like the adults we were. As time went on, we came to this conclusion: Looking back is more like a mindset we have. It's like the person who "had it made" before he or she moved out of their folks' place and is now having to live on his or her own and pay bills for the first time. It's like children that are going from kindergarten to 1st grade, or 8th grade to 9th grade and so on and so on. Change sometimes makes us look back to what we had and will create a want for what we were content or secure with in our past. Some people just don't like change. Some people just like everything like it is, or like it always has been. They have the mindset that "Good is good enough for me." In the forefront of their minds is always a "Why???" or "Why do I" or "Why should I".

> *"Change sometimes makes us look back to what we had and will create a want for what we were content or secure with in our past."*

Lot's wife couldn't understand the change that was taking place in their lives. She had trouble with why she had to leave her beautiful home and land. She didn't want to leave what she had; even though, she was about to be killed if she didn't move. She didn't understand that God was her Father, and He wanted the best for her. Another example is an entire nation of people looking back on what they had once been comfortable with back in their old way of life. You can go back biblically (Exodus 14:12) to the story about the Israelites and find that after they had been delivered from slavery in Egypt and were traveling through the wilderness, they complained. God delivered them from bondage. They had a chance to be free, but when things got tough, they did not act like the "tough got going". It's like the Israelites got held up in the desert and just wanted to quit. They got frustrated and started looking back on the times in Egypt. They thought it was better to serve the Egyptians as slaves than to be free in the place they were. They couldn't see their future because they were looking at their past.

It is important that you look at the changes you are going through and see the hand of God in those changes. The vision and plan He has for you is for you to always be moving forward to better things; and, not to just have it made, but to be in a real relationship with Him.

Despite

"Then his wife said to him, "Do you still hold fast to your integrity? Curse God and die!" Job 2:9 (NKJV)

"Curse God and die," Job's wife said to him in the book of Job. "*Forget it!!! What's the use??!! It doesn't even matter anymore!!!*" These are strong, honest words in the moment of crisis or a state of chaos. Everything is gone! No hope is in sight so why live? These kinds of moments happen in relationships all the time. Whether it's within a family, amongst friends, co-workers, or church members, you name it, anything dealing with people has a chance of failure, and it seems as if there are no apparent or visible reasons for the failures. (I say visible reason because at the time we say, "I can't see why this happened.") There have been times in me and Robyn's life where we lived these moments out. We have lost jobs due to cutbacks, lost a house due to mismanagement of money, and lost a child for an unknown reason. This girl and me have lost some things in our lives that placed us in a position of asking Why God? But we made it through together by God and Him alone. I've turned my back on Robyn, and she turned her back on me. However, as we turned to Him, He would always turn us back to one another because we would be facing Him.

"But he said to her, "You speak as one of the foolish women speaks. Shall we indeed accept good from God, and shall we not accept adversity?" In all this, Job did not sin with his lips." Job 2:10 (NKJV)

Tough times and those words Job spoke were hard to say, and the moment were rough to bear. No one likes to lose; no one welcomes failure. Time and life's continuation provides its own healing; having people around you to give support and encouragement helps. Being alone to mourn for a short moment and knowing that despite everything else, God is a good Father, and He has all the love we need in Him.

In regard to relationships, we were made for them, and they were made for us, despite what they may bring.

One and Onlys

Let me inform you that in this section the "Man" can follow the same path as we see in both Adam and Eve. It is really just a characteristic or personality trait one may have. If the woman is like Adam, it's ok. You are together for a reason, and that reason is to be fruitful and multiply, replenish the earth, subdue it, and to have dominion over everything on earth.

In an *Adam and Eve* relationship, both parties are placed on the earth to *"do"* something together. They should work together because when they don't, they are not fulfilling Gods plan for their lives. Adam was given what he had to do and Eve was placed on the earth to help Adam. What we find in Scripture is, that things became complicated for both of them because they were not together of one mind in their obedience. They were in the same place, but doing separate things. It is like two successful people working at the same place but at different jobs. They can have more fulfillment when they work together. The instructions to Adam and Eve were to be fruitful and multiply (Genesis 1:28*)*. That responsibility requires a same mindedness- a harmony between them.

The Making

Eve (not being gender-based) can be described as a good person, but she can be easily swayed and not in control of anything on her own. She is always dependent on another person. Eve displays the need for another to always be in the lead. She is a co-dependent person.

If a person is a type of "Eve", they don't make the best decisions on their own. They require someone to help them on what to do. There may be some disadvantages when one is in relationship to an Eve. When you are feeling down, they're down. When you are happy, they're happy. They have good hearts and good intentions but sometimes can't see when they're not helping even though they believe that they are helping. They don't know who they are, and they will be whoever you want them to be. In this relationship once they both understand their roles they can be unstoppable because of the authority they were giving.

The Adam type of person must not fail to keep his Eve by his side while he is replenishing the earth and subduing the land. As we can see in this kind of relationship, one person is working and being busy taking care of the home, and the other is really just finding their way through life. They could be finding their way from job to job looking for what's best fits them, or making their way through school, drifting from course to course seeking their real interest, or be a stay at home parent.

In any relationship, circumstances like these can and will be frustrating. All ***frustration*** is an unmet need by a person who is trying to get something they want, but can't get. What Adam has to do is be the lead and stick to God's plan for them, instead of buying into what Eve may be selling with some new idea outside of God's plan for them. Adam has to say things like, "That's not what God said. This is the plan and we are sticking to it. I understand what you may have heard and what you may have seen, but this is the way it will be." Of course that is easier said than done, but it's possible. Trust God that you can do it and say it. Exercise Godliness by going to God and explaining your actions to Him.

I know there had been times in my marriage when my wife and I had just finished discussing our finances and she would go out with her sister and they would find a "b*uy-one-get-one half off*" sale. So she would buy something. Then she would come to me with her *pretty self* and strut around me and ask, *"What do you think?"* Let me tell you how it really went down. She would say, *"Ben, can I model for you?"* and I would say, *"Sure."*

We would be in our room, and I'm sitting on the bed and she would undress in front of me while telling me about her day with her sister. While sitting there, I'm drooling over how good she looks, and paying absolutely no attention to what she was saying. Even with her dressed, I'm looking at her and thinking, *"You should go ahead and take that off."* Then she will say, *"I know what we've talked about, but it was on sale. I'll take it back if I have to take it back."*

Now who was wrong in this situation? Is it the beautiful woman or the drooling man? To me, this is what happened with Adam. Eve walked up and said, *"Hey, taste this."* and Adam said, *"O.K."* I bet he was not looking at the fruit in her hand. *Hello somebody!*

The Making

Things are different now because we both have started to recognize where we messed up and blamed one another. But in these moments you have to be aware of what is at stake and what the consequences are after the decision. In *Adam and Eve's* situation, that one decision changed everything, and I mean <u>EVERYTHING!</u>

As you grow in your relationship with one another, pay attention to each other, when things are heating up or "going south". Ask yourselves, "Are we having an Adam and Eve moment? Have we gotten out of line? Are we doing something wrong? Let's stop, go to God and explain ourselves."

One Purpose

Let's look at the relationship of *Abraham and Sarah*. In this type of relationship, you will have someone, like Abraham, that has been led and saved by God in many occurrences in his life. This relationship is one where God has called the man out from his family to do something different.

Abraham was a man chosen by God and given a great promise that was for a special purpose. Abraham was married to Sarah, who is the one and only woman the promise could come through. To accomplish this, Abraham was told by God to leave his family and his homeland, and to be shown by God to a place he did not know. Abraham had to go to a new place to do this new thing God appointed in the promise (Genesis 12:1-3).

Have you ever been there? You knew what God said. You were obedient to His Word, but for the life of you, you couldn't see how He was going to accomplish it. This is where Abraham was too. He was a man committed to God and convinced that he was being led by God.

[1] "And when Abram was ninety years old and nine, the LORD appeared to Abram, and said unto him, I am the Al-

mighty God; walk before me, and be thou perfect. ² And I will make my covenant between me and thee, and will multiply thee exceedingly." Genesis 17:1-2 (KJV)

He knew that these ideas and thoughts he were having came from a source greater than himself. He just couldn't see how he was to become the father of many nations when he didn't have a son and his wife was a barren woman. But our God is the God of possibilities. When God gives His Word, it is already possible. I've learned from my own experience that if everything I'm doing makes sense, I'm not living by faith. There has to be impossibilities in my life where I'm not depending on myself but on Him. There are so many stories in the Bible of people who lived by faith that their actions made absolutely no sense. I'm sure you know a story or two.

As with Abraham's marriage, you have to have someone like Sarah, someone who will back and follow her husband in everything he is doing. The main thing I want you to take note of is that Sarah played a big part in God's plan for His people. God chose them both. His blessing was upon Abraham and His favor was upon Sarah. Because of the promise they had God's hedge of protection around them. It is God's love and grace that was on Abraham and Sarah. You may not believe it, but there is a high possibility that you and your spouse may have that same love and grace upon your lives.

This scenario was true for me early on in my marriage. I knew my wife would follow me anywhere. I knew this from how she was as my girlfriend and, honestly, it was one of the qualities that drew me to her. But as we started to follow God on a path I knew not of, I got scared. Not because I was afraid of my future, but because of my thinking *"What if I'm wrong?"*

The Relationship

I had no clue where I was going, but I knew I was following God's leading and His voice (The Holy Spirit) -this was new to me.

It would have been different if it was just me and God, but I had Robyn and some kids. If I was wrong, I would be leading them astray. On top of that, I knew me. I knew myself and of all the times I had been wrong and now I have people following and depending on me. All this was new to me, and as of result, I experienced a whole new type of pressure. We would run into what I call "Wye in the Roads" and I had to make the decision to go left or right, stop or stay, or go back. The decision was up to me.

I was being led by God but, "My God it wasn't easy." You would think that following God would be easy, but there are so many things to know and to be aware of that I didn't understand. This is where Wisdom was birthed for me. My Father (God) taught me how to **Stop** and **Go.** When I went too far or went off course, He would tug me back into place. I began to learn the difference between what was my part and what was His part. How to listen and when to speak? He taught me that even when I missed it, He would make things right.

My wife played a huge part in it also. I would go to her and say, "I don't know where to go or what to do. I need you to be praying for us that I make the right decision." There were times when we both were insecure in our actions, but we got over that insecurity as time went by. There were some times where she would criticize me (in my mind☺) and my decisions and I would have to say, "Hey I need you to stop acting like everyone around me and start acting like my wife and not a critic." I know I was hard on her in the beginning because it was hard for me. Yet, as I learned how to rephrase what I said, she learned how to **Listen** and not just to me, but to God, which was another huge benefit to me having her backing me up. I Love my wife, and she loves me – we love God. Things haven't been easy, but we have sure had some adventures with God.

Just like with Abraham and Sarah, our relationship is also special. We realize that we could not accomplish our God-given, Life's Purpose without each other. The Abraham and Sarah relationship is almost the easiest to fix and if you have one, just be honest with each other. Have the common goal of communication that communicates, "Hey, I need you, and you need me. Let's make this work, not for the kids, not for the house, not for our folks, but because of God's Will and Promise." Let that be your primary reason and then everyone and everything else will follow suit and be blessed because of it.

Us or *Him*, but somebody has to go, and we choose *Him*

People sometimes find themselves in situations where it is not so much the devil, but their own actions. Some of the problems that come to us are because of us. They come as a result of our wants and desires, needs and greed and our ambitions and goals – situations that cause us to feel discontented. Situations that may even cause us to even question our marriage or any other relationship. As a word of caution, I warn you that there will be times you may think, *"Here I am with this person, but I would rather be with someone else?"* Or *"Why am I here and not somewhere else?"* Or *why am I doing this while I can be doing that – yet, you know that God's plan for you is to stay with them and stay where you are and do what you're doing."* These thoughts may come when we listen to that little anxious voice that tries to convince us to make the wrong decision when doing the right thing.

As a word of encouragement, there is a defense you can recognize. That being convinced that God has already established a plan and a purpose for you, and it's for both you and your spouse.

11

Two of a Kind

¹ "But a certain man named Ananias, with Sapphira his wife, sold a possession, ² And kept back part of the price, his wife also being privy to it, and brought a certain part, and laid it at the apostles' feet." Acts 5:1&2 (KJV)

In this relationship, you can find two people fully in agreement, but to a flaw. This relationship has many different angles to view. You may be able to see Ananias as an overbearing husband that no one could tell him anything because he was a *know it all*. Or, you can look at them as having the old *Bonnie and Clyde* kind of relationship, the ride or die couple, which is desirable to an extent.

Ananias and Sapphira, are a lot like Abraham and Sarah but without the guidance of the Holy Spirit. They didn't know when to intercede: when to say no, when to go to God for an overbearing husband or wife for help, and then to believe that they are doing right by God by submitting to one another.

We can look at the relationships we have already talked about and see how Adam should have done the same thing with

The Making

Eve. He saw what she was doing, and he knew better. He was not blind to it by any means; after all, he knew what God said. Sapphira wasn't either. She saw and knew what her husband was doing.

"But Peter said, "Ananias, why has Satan filled your heart to lie to the Holy Spirit and keep back part of the price of the land for yourself?" Acts 5:3 (NKJV)

Not to meddle in anyone's business, but this can happen in instances such as with taxes, resumes, applications or any small little white lie. Little white lies with quick benefits but with life-long consequences that if you had just told the truth you would have had either the same return or outcome. However, because of greed and unwise decision making, you lose it all because of fear to speak up because you didn't know how to do what you knew to do. The moral of the story in this relationship is for you to be careful and do the right thing. Many times, in relationships such as marriage, because one person decides not to voice their opinions, they both suffer in the end.

This brings us to, *"What do I do when I don't know how to do what I know to do?"* How does the submitted wife speak up to a know-it-all husband? How does the husband explain why his daughter is the way she is to his wife, when his wife is saying, *"I am a woman and you are a man, so how can you tell me about my daughter?"*

We all have been in this situation; perhaps at work with a bad boss, or as children trying to warn their parents. I have learned the best way to handle the situation is to say, *"You will thank me later,"* and then tell them what I believe to be true. I have learned that giving it to them *short and sweet* is the best

The Relationship

way. The other person will be upset for a moment, but they will eventually get over it. We must learn the importance of our role in the relationship. You are there for a reason and so is the other person. We must learn to work together.

Remember, another goal for you while reading this book is for you to be able to think of your own solutions and figure out what will work best for you. I understand that not every relationship is the same, so there may be many different ways that will work for you. I believe that you two have to find the "*shoes that fit*" and walk in the path of righteousness.

Three-Way Love Affair

¹ "I am the rose of Sharon, And the lily of the valleys. ² Like a lily among thorns, So is my love among the daughters. ³Like an apple tree among the trees of the woods, So is my beloved among the sons. I sat down in his shade with great delight, And his fruit was sweet to my taste." Song of Solomon 2:1-3 (NKJV)

In this scripture, there are three people being portrayed: Jesus, a woman and a man. I found this scripture one day after I asked God how I should view my marriage because I knew that Robyn and I were different. Not better, just different. I believe that everyone on earth is different. I believe we should all see ourselves that way; Jesus does, even though we are all God's children.

So my wife and I took the scripture to heart. I see her as a lily among thorns, meaning compared to other women, she stands out. She is alive and beautiful. She sees me as an apple tree among the trees in the woods, which is to say I am a radiant, tall tree with large branches and big red delicious apples. Together, "we" see Jesus as the Rose of Sharon, meaning He is our focal point, despite everything going on around us. We

The Making

look for the life that can only be found in Him. We keep our focus on Him **TOGETHER**. I see her, she sees me, and we see Him. If we don't, things will go wrong.

In the book of Songs of Solomon, Solomon expresses his love for his love. They describe their experiences with one another and how they feel when away from one another. They describe the feelings they have while waiting for one another. To me, this is the way we should express our love for one another. A man that expresses and describes his need for his love and explains his wants and desires for her. A woman who isn't ashamed to say, "I need you. I miss you and I'll do anything to and for you."

As you can tell, this section is for grown folks, preferably married folks, those who are honest, open, and understanding.

The 1 + 1 = 2 kind of folks.
A relationship worth keeping kind of folks.
2 people chasing 1 God kind of folks.

The type of folks we all should be like… kind of folks. We can all have this type of relationship. We just have to open up and be honest. It will probably make you feel vulnerable, but this kind of vulnerability is good for you. It's the picture of two people taking turns falling back into each other's arms as a sign of trust. I also believe we all deserve a relationship like this. I am not going to teach you how because that is God's part, but I will tell you this: that it is possible to have, and that you can do it.

I know that there are many distractions and temptations out there.

"So humble yourselves before God. Resist the devil, and he will flee from you." James 4:7 (NLT)

We as men have to learn how to cleave to our wives and do our own thing. Woman, pray for your man, and if you're already praying, continue to pray for him. He needs your prayers. After you get done praying listen to what he has to say; if he doesn't say much pray again, and be patient, the Holy Spirit will tell you what to do. This is easier said than done, but it is possible. One of my favorite sayings is from Bob Marley, *"If she's amazing, she won't be easy. If she's easy, she won't be amazing. If she's worth it, you won't give up. If you give up, you're not worthy."*

So, my friends, when it comes to having a *Solomon* and his lover relationship, it is possible, it is doable, but you have to be open, honest, and willing. Remember that temptations will come, so be aware and on guard, because relationships are for grown folks.

The Ultimate Relationship

Just as Christ so loved the church and gave Himself for her.

This is by far one of the most recited Bible verses for married couples, and by far one of the most hardest things for a couple to come to grips with. This is the picture-perfect ideal relationship. It sounds sweet and honorable like it should have music playing in the background with doves flying all around you as you walk or sit with your spouse. But hey, let's be honest here, have you ever known a woman that was so excited to SUBMIT to her husband all the time?

The woman that would be like, "I just love it when he tells me what to do like cook this or clean that, and do that too. I love waking up every morning ready to wait on him hand and foot… I LOVE going places and cooking for his family. My life is great because of him!" ☺ Or what about the man? Have you ever met a man that loves to stay home all the time and carry the load and never do anything for himself? A man who says, "No, I'll never need a man cave; we'll make that your sewing room. No, no, no scratch that babe, let me make it a shoe room. I'll build you as many shelves as you need right after we get back

The Making

from shopping.

I've never met a woman that is "tickled fancy" to do everything her man says... never! Or a man who couldn't get enough of spending time and doing stuff for his woman, like he didn't have a life of his own. The Bible says in Ephesians 5, 21-29 (NLT),

[21]"And further, submit to one another out of reverence for Christ. [22]For wives, this means submit your husbands as to the Lord. [23]For a husband is the head of his wife as Christ is the head of the church. He is the Savior of his body, the church. [24]As the church submits to Christ, so you wives should submit to your husbands in everything. [25]For husbands, this means love your wives, just as Christ loved the church. He gave his life for her [26]to make her holy and clean, washed by the cleansing of God's word. [27]He did this to present her to himself as a glorious church without a spot or wrinkle or any other blemish. Instead, she will be holy and without fault. [28]In the same way, husbands ought to love their wives as they love their own bodies. For a man who loves his wife actually shows love for himself. [29]No one hates his own body but feeds and cares for it, just as Christ cares for the church."

Listen, we are all humans. We all have a mind of our own. However, as a married couple, we have to keep each other accountable as we each follow and grow in Christ. It is hard, but it is doable and rewarding at the same time, if we faint not. It's important that we find out what works best for us and our relationship.

In this Ultimate Relationship, we must do what is best for *US*, not ME or HIM or HER, but US, WE. "Just Me and You",

The Relatioship

like the song by Tony Toni Tone (look it up I know you got your phone on you). We must understand that we are together and that we must both be respectful to one another and not expect our mate to make a one-hundred (100) on every test. We must understand that both of us are growing and changing, physically and mentally, and hopefully spiritually.

Look at it from this perspective, a woman is dealing with a man who was formed from the dirt. He has no good in him, but he is learning and stumbling and fumbling his way after God in life. Going off of what he believes is the right thing to do for his family. The man is dealing with a church (his wife), and we all know that the church is full of different characters, personalities and mindsets.

There is no such thing as a perfect person. For someone to say that he or she is looking for that perfect person is like me saying I want to get my daughter a pink and white Unicorn for her birthday. Everyone has heard of Unicorns or seen pictures of them, but they don't exist. It would be nice to have, but I will never find one.

We must clear the air and release each other from the expectation of the responsibility that comes with our titles and look at one another as: they're doing their best while they are learning how to do the right thing. I wouldn't just sit and settle for whatever, but I would suggest to you to be a little less harsh on the situation. *Be open minded and understanding. Don't be a fool and don't be too much, just be enough.*

The only thing perfect is The Word of God. All we can do is believe in Him and live a life in Christ with the Grace that has been given freely to us. Look at one another, talk honestly and

The Making

openly with one another with understanding, with forgiveness, and have accountability for our actions.

Having an Ultimate Relationship is possible. It's just going to take a lot of togetherness and time spent in the Word.

Things to try for the Ultimate Relationship

Talk to one another.
Write to one another.
Text to one another.
Listen openly to one another.
Help one another.
Love one another.

I know no one likes to be told what to do. Just be you and try it out. Remember, don't buy shoes that don't fit.   -Ben

THE MINISTER

A Minister is
One who acts
under the authority
of another,
a servant,
an attendant.
To give things
that are needed,
to minister to ones needs.

The Making

You may not know it, but you have been ministering all your life, and you have been ministered to your entire life. Don't think that a minister is just someone you see in the pulpit on Sunday morning, or ministry is something done at church. Both are a way of life.

As you read the remainder of this book, try and look at ministering from a different angle- a more personal level, then and ask yourself the following questions:

- Who have I been ministering to?
- Who has been ministering to me?
- What type of minister Am I?
- When do I minister and don't know it?
- What is now expected and demanded of me?

The Cost

The Cost of following Christ

⁵⁷"As they were walking along, someone said to Jesus, "I will follow you wherever you go." ⁵⁸But Jesus replied, "Foxes have dens to live in, and birds have nests, but the Son of Man has no place even to lay his head." ⁵⁹He said to another person, "Come, follow me." The man agreed, but he said, "Lord, first let me return home and bury my father." ⁶⁰But Jesus told him, "Let the spiritually dead bury their own dead! Your duty is to go and preach about the Kingdom of God." ⁶¹Another said, "Yes, Lord, I will follow you, but first let me say good-bye to my family." ⁶²But Jesus told him, "Anyone who puts a hand to the plow and then looks back is not fit for the Kingdom of God." Luke 9:57-62 (NLT)

Have you ever heard the statement that nothing in life is free, or everything has a price? The man who loves his life will lose it while the man who hates his life in this world will keep his life in eternity.

Everything has its price, either with the exchange of money; your time, effort or life in general, there is always an exchange of something either good or bad. There is always a price.

The Making

Keep this in mind before you accept the call. When it comes to being a *minister*, you have to give up something for the better benefit of others. It can be either with a church, man to his wife, a wife to her husband, parent to a child, or a child to a parent.

Everyone does something for someone else. Accepting the call to be either a husband or wife, church leader or community leader or whatever your case may be, understand that there will be some things that you will have to lay down. For me, as a father, I had to stop everything: taking trips, buying clothes, and hanging out with the fellas. I had to count the cost before I could continue on. It wasn't good for me to keep hanging out with my friends, my brother, my uncles or my cousins. As a husband it was something that I had to lay down and pick up. I had to learn how to be and stay with one woman and focus all my attention towards her and allow all my needs to be fulfilled through her. I understand that the Bible says that God will supply all our needs and above our needs through His riches and Glory, but I am a man, and I have needs. God created the Birds and the Bees for a reason. ***Any Who***...there were some things I had to learn. As a follower of Christ, there were more things I had to learn and one thing I had to lay down, and that was my life.

I want to encourage you to not get discouraged when counting the cost for your future. Jesus asked this question, "And what do you benefit if you gain the whole world but lose your soul." Mark 8:36 (NLT) I'll be honest there will be a lot of things that you will see as losses up front. However, in the tail end, you will see the impact that you made on those around you. I believe it is one of the best decisions one can make.

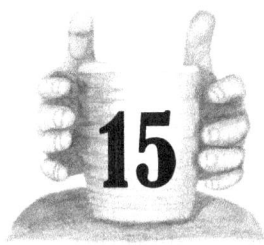

The Hand You Have

Having a royal flush is every poker player's dream. A once in a lifetime hand that beats all other hands is the way most people want to live their lives. They want the perfect mate with the perfect job, so they can have perfect kids in the perfect neighborhood, with perfect neighbors, attending a perfect church ten miles down the road, while living the perfect life. The businessman or woman wants a perfect business plan, with a perfect team of perfect people to make a perfect business that runs perfectly.

In most cases this never happens. All card players get a bad hand every now and then. Anyone looking for that perfect person will run into a hand full of jokers, and we all know this. The thing we all have to remember is what are we learning from these losses? What should I have not done? What could I have done?

These are all important questions but what I'm really after is: How do you win with what seems to be a losing situation? How do you win with a mate who doesn't appear to want to do anything or go anywhere? Or, how do you win when your kids

The Making

are acting like your family members or people you know? How do you win with the hand you have been dealt?

Most leaders, coaches, or bosses know what it takes to be a winner. You have to have all the right ingredients to have a winning anything.

When most people look at their hand, they see all the weakest links (which are usually people) first. It could be a husband looking down on a wife or a wife looking down on a husband. But whatever the case may be, you have to work with what you have.

Many times you are stuck in an impossible position, but for God to get the glory, you just have to make do for a season. If you are wise enough to be quiet and not curse what God is blessing you with, you will have the result that you want. However, if you sit there and complain and "bad talk" your situation, you will have what you say.

"But we have only five loaves of bread and two fish!" they answered." Matthew 14:17 (NLT)

In this verse, Jesus made do with what he had to meet the needs of those there with him. He fed more than 5,000 people with 2 fish and 5 loaves of bread. I don't think the disciples talked bad about what he was doing because they didn't have time to. They had never seen anything like that done before and, on top of that, they had leftovers! Whenever God blesses you with a meal and you have leftovers, just know that God blessed you.

Remember this:
When God blesses you, you have extra.

When God provides for you, you have enough.

So, how do you win with the hand you have? You make due with what you have. You continue to play your hand. Continue to learn yourself: who you are and what you're capable of doing. Don't quit and throw in your hand. Listen: No one has the blueprint for your life. No one can tell you how everything is going to play out. I haven't found anywhere in the Bible where God Himself told anyone how everything was going to end up when He was calling on them to do a faith walk of just believing and trusting Him.

Let me encourage you to continue and seek God and His righteousness. Read and study His Word. You don't have to study anything you may be going through at the time, just read something. It doesn't have to be a lot of reading, just enough to make you think about Him. Play your hand and stay in the game, and one day you'll get that royal flush.

Know Your Moment

"To everything there is a season, a time for every purpose under heaven." Ecclesiastes 3:1 (NKJV)

Knowing your moment is very important. However, many times we don't know when it's our time. There are a lot of people that wing it and look like they know what they are doing, and yet, they really don't. Knowing your moment can be one of the hardest things to recognize if you don't pay attention to the signs and know the times that you're in.

Yes, we all would like to be in the happy moments of life, such as graduation, buying a new house or car, first day on the job, or looking down at your newborn baby in the crib. Everyone loves those moments. But, what about the moment's right before you decide what subject to take at college, or should I own or rent, or should I apply for this job or stay at my current job, or maybe even, are we really ready for kids? Should we really get married? In these moments– in the time of making lifelong decisions– take a moment before you answer.

Time after time, people make lifelong decisions in the mo-

The Making

ment. The Bible says in Ecclesiastes 3:11 that God has made everything beautiful in HIS time. Here are 4 moments to be aware of:

Positioning
Positioning by definition is to be put into correct location.

"He makes me to lie down in green pastures; He leads me beside the still waters." Psalms 23:2 (NKJV)

As believers, we are filled with the Spirit and led by the Spirit. There will be times when we will be placed in situations that we wouldn't have normally placed ourselves, but we are there for a reason. It could be a job, a church, or a place to stay. God placed you there for a reason. There is something you must learn or do and sometimes you will learn what not to do. And that's the only place you are to do it in, and unfortunately, no one can tell you why. In this place, you have to ask God why and, through that, you will develop your relationship with Him. This will make the reason more meaningful because you will know that you know, and no one can take that away from you or tell you otherwise. Trust and growth are essential in positioning.

Pruning
Pruning by definition is to lop or cut off to trim; to clean.

"Every branch in Me that does not bear fruit He takes away; and every branch that bears fruit He prunes, that it may bear more fruit." John 15:2 (NKJV)

No one likes to be pruned, but at times God will cut things back for you so that you can produce more of His goodness in your life. He usually does this when everything is just like you believe things should be.

I'm not talking about like what happened to Job where you may lose something valuable to you, like a family member, property, your health or things tied to a dream of yours coming true. I am talking about a demotion or a "Pink-Slip" on a job, or something along those lines.

As believers, we go from Faith to Faith and Glory to Glory. We go from place to place, from this-to-that and from here to there. We are always moving. Jesus never stood still. He never stayed in only one place; He never did just one miracle. Jesus never thought He had made it.

When it comes to pruning for the better, it always seems to look like it's a waste of time. However, pruning is a lot like circumcision, the cutting away of something that will be in the way later. I can remember as a little boy growing up in the country, my dad and I would go to my grandmother's and clean her yard for her. I would cut the grass and my dad would cut the hedges. One year he said to me, *"B, we need to prune the limbs off this tree so that it can grow better this spring."* I said, *"Prune it for it to grow? It looks like its growing fine to me."* He said, *"It does, but it's a Crape Myrtle Tree. If we go ahead and prune it this year, it will be able to grow and be much fuller this time next year."* I thought to myself, yeah if we leave it alone it would be even that much fuller this time next year.

Looking at my face, he said, *"B, if we leave it alone it will, over time over crowd itself and begin to kill itself because of its heavy limbs. Those limbs will cover up the ground and not allow enough sunlight to shine on it, that too will cause it to die slowly."*

The Making

So we cut the tree back to what looked to me bare but he said it was "just right". I thought to myself, "*You just killed a perfectly beautiful tree that was growing fine until we touched it with our bush cutters.*"

My dad said to me, "*You'll see next year why I pruned it.*" My grandmother didn't mind so I just kept quiet. A year went by and, lo and behold, the tree did grow back. The flowers bloomed and the tree was beautiful again. I learned a very valuable lesson that year, and that was, despite what I may think, it's ok to cut back some things even though they don't look necessary.

I want to encourage you to not bug out when things change. He will work it out. Just be patient, calm down, relax, ask God, read His word and continue to grow.

Conditioning

Conditioning by definition is to make; to form; to limit or restrict, to put in fit or proper state.

"I will bless those who bless you, And I will curse him who curses you; And in you all the families of the earth shall be blessed." Genesis 12:3 (NKJV)

As believers, we were made to be doers, lovers and rulers. However, before all of that, we have to be conditioned. Before someone is a soldier, he or she has to go through boot camp and before 1st grade you have to go through kindergarten. Before college, there is high school. Before working a job, there is an orientation. Before every new beginning, there is a time when you have to be conditioned for the next phase of life. So there is no way to avoid it.

The Minister

What I want you to do is approach the situation with knowledge and understanding, so that it will be easier to get through. Here's a Bible verse that is familiar to many: *"Weeping may endure for a night, but joy comes in the morning."* Many of us know this scripture right… Wrong! Many people misquote this verse. This scripture is a big deal to me. Why? Because if you read Psalm 30 in full, you will get a full understanding of what it is saying.

"For His anger is but for a moment, His favor is for life; Weeping may endure for a night, but joy comes in the morning." Psalms 30:5 (NKJV)

Many times in our lives we say things we learned from people and we don't know what we are really saying. I want to encourage you to read the Bible on your own and ask the Holy Spirit to help you, that's what He is there for.

Many times we go over and over things that we really don't have to continue to go over repeatedly. If we learn how to avoid bad turns and just pay attention, we will know when it is our moment to turn from the pattern of doing the same things over and over. So, back to the weeping that we endure for a night statement, many people quote this when they're going through hard times and yes, hard times will come, the Bible tells about it when it says in Ecclesiastes:

"In the day of prosperity be joyful, But in the day of adversity consider: Surely God has appointed the one as well as the other, So that man can find out nothing that will come after him." Ecclesiastes 7:14 (NKJV)

In those hard and difficult moments, be strong and focused,

but don't continue to be foolish. Remember at the beginning of Psalms 30:5, "… for his anger is but for a moment" meaning He may be mad at some of your actions (think about what you did or what you should have done) and know that His favor is for life. He chastises you as a son because He loves you. I'm just saying, it could be something you may be overlooking that is causing you all this stress or self-inflicting problems.

You know how it is in relationships, someone may stop talking because their mate didn't pay attention to their hair, dress, and makeup: or at a clean car, grass that has been cut, or a made-up bed. It goes both ways.

Any Who! Sometimes God wants us to acknowledge Him in our ways, but when we get caught up in doing our own thing sometimes He stops speaking for us to notice that we can't hear Him anymore. I want to encourage you to pay attention while you are being conditioned into the man or woman that God is making. Remember what He said in Jeremiah 18:6, He is the Potter and we are the clay, He is conditioning us.

"O house of Israel, cannot I do with you as this potter? saith the LORD. Behold, as the clay is in the potter's hand, so are ye in mine hand, O house of Israel." Jeremiah 18:6 (KJV)

Transforming

Transforming by definition means to change in form or appearance; metamorphosis, to change in condition, nature or character; convert.

"And do not be conformed to this world, but be transformed by the renewing of your mind, that you may prove what is that good and acceptable and perfect will of God." Romans 12:2 (NKJV)

Going from one thing to an entirely different thing, while being the same thing at the same time. You've seen the movie "Transformers" how a car changes (transforms) to a fighting machine. Or you've seen that a caterpillar becomes a butterfly. Likewise, the Sinner is changed to a Believer.

We humans are unique in that we have a mind, a will, and intellect. As we go thru life we change physically, emotionally, and intellectually. The physical form of us changes while our emotions adjust with our maturity, and our intellect increases with our learning. Even so, we continue to be human, just as we were created to be. We are constantly going thru some type of transformation.

The apostle Paul has to be in the top ten characters in the Bible who made the biggest change in his life by God transforming him into a new person. Transforming is a beautiful thing. One day you wake up and you're different. You can't explain why, but you know it happened, and you're the better for it. I won't go into detail about transforming because we all transform differently, and that's o.k. You be you, and that is o.k.

Another beautiful thing about transforming is that you don't have to do anything for it. It just happens. It is nothing you have to work for or work on, God does it all, just accept His grace and you will be fine.

"Being confident of this very thing, that he which hath begun a good work in you will perform it until the day of Jesus Christ." Philippians 1:6 (KJV)

As you are made into the minister you are supposed to be, just continue on and Be Made.

THE GREAT COMEBACK

Why Believe

Looking For What Once Was

"But they found the stone rolled away from the tomb. Then they went in and did not find the body of the Lord Jesus." Luke 24:2-3 (NKJV)

Many times in our lives, we will look for Christ in places where *we* believe He should be. We will look in churches, on TV, or in people; anywhere for some kind of evidence of the Lord, yet, we won't find Him there, not the way we perceive Him to *Be* anyway.

It is in those moments of searching that we have to keep up the faith and continue to look for Him. We must be mindful of Him, lest we become taken just like what happened to His disciples. They lost hope because they couldn't find Him in the place where they last saw Him. We have to be fully convinced in what He said, and that is He would never leave us or forsake us.

Hoping For What Could Have Been

The Making

The great thing about His coming back is that He was right there with them in their unbelief.

"But we were hoping that it was He who was going to redeem Israel. Indeed, besides all this, today is the third day since these things happened." Luke 24:21 (NKJV)

The disciples here have thrown in the towel on what they used to believe in, due to what they knew by nature. From what the disciples had been taught, they knew two things. First, what Jesus had been telling them for three years about the Kingdom of God; and second, how the Son of God was going to have to suffer for the redemption of Israel. They envisioned and anticipated the presence of a Leader, a King, to be among them. But what happened? They began to look at the tomb and thought their hopes and dreams where gone. Thus, their hopes turned into doubts.

Life lesson for the day: Listen to what God is telling you instead of what you are telling yourself. What gets us into more trouble than anything else is listening to ourselves, mainly when God is teaching us something new. We tend to voice our opinion and put doubt on something we should be sure of. For example, in Luke 1:18 (NLT), the Bible states, "Zechariah said to the angel, "How can I be sure this will happen? I'm an old man now, and my wife is also well along in years."

As believers we have to recognize our moment.

Your Great Comeback

Right before The Great Comeback happened, everyone was hopeless. Then Jesus came back and filled them with the Holy Spirit to be their comforter. The Great Comeback is for you:

1. God has saved you.
2. God has encamped His angels around you as a hedge of protection.
3. God has filled you with His Holy Spirit to guide you into All Truth.

You, Sir or Ma'am, are equipped to Be. You are equipped to Be the thing He wants you to be and sent you to be. As the old church folks would say, "Say Amen to that Church!"

I would like to encourage you once again. This is my book and what I wrote is my story. I believe if you are a reader then that, also, makes you a writer. Write your own story; write your own opinions, your own experiences, and your viewpoints. Write down what you know to be true to you and share it. Share it in love, share it in hope, and share it for the Glory of God.

The Making

Let's start being the answer to the WWJD question. If you are young, you may have missed that era of wristbands and necklaces. WWJD means, "What Would Jesus Do?"

The Great Comeback is for you making it back to your "First love". Back to where you believe again.

"I know your works, your labor, your patience, and that you cannot bear those who are evil. And you have tested those who say they are apostles and are not, and have found them liars; and you have persevered and have patience, and have labored for My name's sake and have not become weary. Nevertheless I have this against you, that you have left your first love." Revelation 2:2-3 (NKJV)

Verse 6 of the above scripture goes on to say that He is doing this in your favor, so don't let the devil play you as a fool. Get back to the person you use to be; Hoping, Waiting, and Believing again!

God wants you back, and He is sending His Son back again for you, but until then we have to be about our Father's business and love again, and then continue to love.

God wants you back in His presence. In a place where Jesus speaks and you hear His voice. Just like when Jesus returned to His disciples, as they were heading back home after finding out that He was gone.

"And they said to one another, "Did not our heart burn within us while He talked with us on the road, and while He opened the Scriptures to us?" Luke 24:32 (NKJV)

The Great Comeback

Right at the place where their hope was given back to them and their hope was brought back to life, in the place where faith is birthed, the place of worship and joy. The place where their **mission** was giving to them by their **commander**. A place of **grace**, which is filled with **faith**. A place where **life** is given. A **place** and **time** for **purpose**. The moment when Frankenstein got up from the table kind of place. A place where someone was brought back to life by a defibrillator. A place where Jordon or LeBron makes the game tying shot, a place when the tables turn, the lights come back on and a miracle has taken place. One of those "But God" moments, or an "If it had not been for the Lord" moments. One of the moments that will never be forgotten. It is when the hourglass has been reset on life. The old song "The Thrill is Gone" by B.B. King has stop being played. The moment of new beginnings. The moment where you can perform everything that you've been taught to do, your <u>instructions</u> and <u>directions.</u>

The moments where unfortunately many believers don't get to enjoy, even though it is given freely to us. Jesus died on the cross for us. *Stop saying I am nothing, stop believing you are worthless.* Jesus didn't give His life for nothing; He gave it for **you!**

We as believers have to get to a place where we stop allowing the devil to steal, kill, and destroy our lives, and if it's not him, we got to stop doing it to ourselves. I want to encourage you that you don't have to be rich to be happy. You don't have to have it all to be happy. It is possible to have Christ in your life and be happy without the bells and whistles that the people of the world have. Just be encouraged that everything God told *you, you* can **have** and **do**. Not what He promised someone else or gave to someone else, but what He told or shown you.

The Making

We're all different. We all have a plan for our lives and it's different from anyone else's. There's only one you; we as believers must have our own sense of independence. Independence by definition means freedom from subjections to the influence or control of others, the state of being independent, which means not relying on others; acting and thinking for oneself, under GOD.

So as we sum-up this Great Comeback, I want you to reflect on this book. I hope that you enjoyed it and I pray that it made some kind of sense to you. It's been an honor to tell you my story, because in the end, it's His Story.

Put on the shoes that fit and give the others away. Allow the Word of God to be a light unto your path as you walk through this life with Christ.

With Much Love, Ben

Conversation Starter:

WARNING: Don't Do This Conversation Starter if you can't handle it. Stop right where you are and do it later. Enjoy the book, talk about the book and get each other's views on the book. Talk about your past experiences, things you like, happy stuff, Real stuff, and Personal stuff. But if either one of you has the slightest feeling of "not readiness," Don't Do It! I would rather you read through this conversation starter alone and think about it by yourself and make a decision. Don't just do it because it's here. This scale is a conversation starter, not a deal breaker. It can show your mate how you really feel and can give you both a goal to reach. It is simply something that you can both use to help and comfort each other.

A huge factor in a relationship is the comfort level. The comfort level in a marriage plays a big part on how each of you gets along with the other, what you talk about, how you spend most of your time together and where you go together. Comfort is very important to have because it has a lot to do with the longevity of a relationship and again, this conversation starter is to help with becoming open with each other. You will find many places where you can stop and talk about things that you wouldn't usually talk about with each other. I believe it is possible to have the best marriage ever, so my wife and I are still working toward that one. We also know how it feels that if things don't change we are on the brink of divorce. We both believe that we are supposed to be together but we also know that if God isn't in our midst that this isn't going to work. So I would recommend you keeping your focus on God, helping each other; being respectful to each other's feelings, and not getting mad when the truth comes.

Notes

Conversation Starter

On a scale of 1 to 10, how would you rate your marriage? 7 and 2 are for you to fill in your own feelings about your marriage.

10: THE BEST MARRIAGE EVER.

9: HAPPILY MARRIED.

8: WE'LL BE FINE ONCE WE GET PAST THE TRUST ISSUE

7: _____

6: WE GOT A LOT OF GROWING TO DO.

5: I'M JUST HERE FOR THE KIDS.

4: IF I COULD, I WOULD BE DOING THIS WITH SOMEONE ELSE

3: I DON'T CARE ANYMORE.

2: _____

1: IF THIS DOESN'T CHANGE, WE ARE ON THE BRINK OF DIVORSE

Ben Freeman, Jr. is the loving husband to Robyn and devoted, proud dad of five wonderful children. He is a first time author, who is excited to share the wisdom God has given him with other married couples who want to do all they can to stay together and make their marriage work. His favorite song growing up was "I'm Just a Nobody" by the Williams Brothers. Ben identified with the "Nobody" of that song. Now he is just trying to tell everybody about somebody who can save anybody.

www.greatlineage.com
ben@greatlineage.com

www.ingramcontent.com/pod-product-compliance
Lightning Source LLC
Chambersburg PA
CBHW070545300426
44113CB00011B/1797